SEPTEMBER

Monday	Tuesday	Wednesday	Thursday	Friday
This summer I had the most fun…	I worry about…	Draw and describe your classroom from your desk.	You are sitting with friends around a campfire telling scary stories. Suddenly you see the bushes move.	Alliteration is the repetition of a beginning sound for effect. *Brown bears burrow below boulders.* Write six.
I'd like you to meet my family. First, there is…	I'd like to ask my teacher these questions about herself/himself.	Write as many things as you can about yourself —your likes, dislikes, favorite things.	Remember a conversation you heard or took part in. Try to write it exactly as it was spoken.	In the first two weeks of school I have learned…
What decisions are you allowed to make at home?	Give an example of how the idiom "Haste makes waste" applies to you.	Did you spend any time last summer looking for falling stars? Write about a nature experience you've had.	Write as much as you know about your state.	Describe how today. Be as s you ca
This past weekend I…	A man is giving away baby elephants. You want one. Convince your parents you need a pet elephant.	Comment on being the oldest, youngest, middle or only child.	Describe a friend — how you met, how you became friends, what you like about each other.	On the firs school this

Name _____   Skill: Writing from experience

Summer Memories

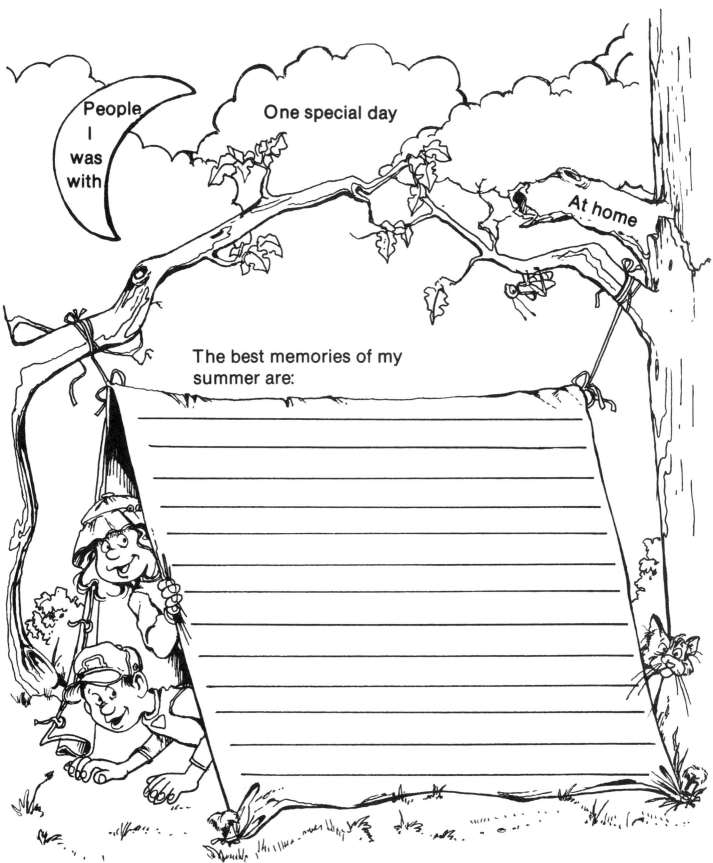

People I was with

One special day

At home

The best memories of my summer are:

_____
_____
_____
_____
_____
_____
_____
_____
_____
_____

Brainwork! Write a paragraph about one of the memories you listed.

OCTOBER

Monday	Tuesday	Wednesday	Thursday	Friday
You enter a time machine. What year is it? What is happening?	The happiest day in my life was…	Compile a "wish list" beginning each sentence with "I wish…"	What kind of sense of humor do you have? Describe an incident that illustrates your sense of humor.	If I were five years older…
Write about something you wouldn't want to give up. Explain.	Give as much information as you can about your favorite movie.	It all started when…	Write about a favorite place.	Explain what you have learned in math since school started in September.
If I could be any character on TV, I would be… because…	The hardest thing I ever had to do was…	Rewrite a past event that didn't work out the way you wanted. Make it work out better.	Pretend you can talk with an animal. What is the animal? What questions would you ask?	As cold as ice As noisy as… As busy as… Write five similes of your own.
Write about your favorite sport or game.	Describe someone in your family.	Write a story using these words: *thunder, electricity, storm, alone, night, telephone,* and *sounds.*	Someone dared you to sleep in the old, haunted house. You accept.	A past Halloween I remember well was…

© Frank Schaffer Publications, Inc.

FS-32012 Writing

Name _____ Skill: Recalling and describing a past emotion

Leaf Back Through Time

Think of a time when you were very happy, very sad, very lonely, or very proud. Describe that time.

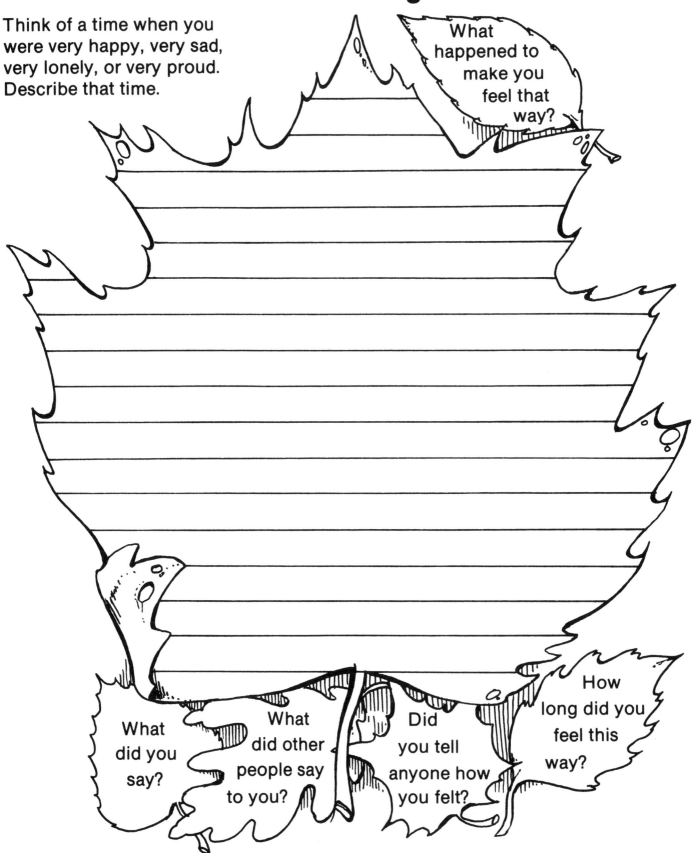

What happened to make you feel that way?

What did you say?

What did other people say to you?

Did you tell anyone how you felt?

How long did you feel this way?

Brainwork! Continue your writing on another leaf-shaped page.

NOVEMBER

Monday	Tuesday	Wednesday	Thursday	Friday
What do you remember about kindergarten or first grade?	Discuss an embarrassing or funny moment in your life or in someone else's.	Persuade your class to try sky diving, or some other exciting sport.	If you could be anyone other than yourself who would you be? Why?	What is your Saturday morning routine?
What would you do if you saw some kids mistreating a dog?	When I'm at home, I like to...	Explain, as if to a new student, what you learned in a recent science lesson.	How do you show your parents you love them?	I was surprised that I...
What do you do when you're home sick? What do you like to eat and drink?	My last birthday was great! First...	Today I feel...	What is the hardest thing for you to do? Explain.	Write about something you did that made you feel good.
The funniest thing I ever saw was...	Describe the most interesting person you have ever met.	Describe everything you ate at Thanksgiving dinner.	Describe how your life might change if there were no TV.	Write a thank-you note to the person who prepared your Thanksgiving meal.

© Frank Schaffer Publications, Inc.

FS-32012 Writing

Name _____   Skill: Writing a letter

Thank you — Letter Perfect

Write a thank-you letter to someone who is important to you.

a b c d e f g h i j k l m   *n o p q r s t u v w x y z*

A B C D E

- What did this person do to help you?
- How did you show your thanks?
- What would you like to do for this person?
- What have you done for this person?
- What will make this person smile?

Brainwork! Draw a picture of yourself and this person on the back of your paper.

© Frank Schaffer Publications, Inc.   FS-32012 Writing

DECEMBER

Monday	Tuesday	Wednesday	Thursday	Friday
Write a holiday story for a child in the first grade.	Write an account of an imaginary or real class trip. Include *who*, *where*, *when*, *how*, and *what*.	Today I learned…	My feelings are easily hurt when…	Relate a scary dream.
Describe one of the best presents you ever received. Why did it make you happy?	What present have you given that made someone happy? Explain.	Over winter vacation I'm going to…	Write about things to do on a snowy day.	Describe things you enjoy. "The first yummy bite of a hot fudge sundae."
Create a fictional classmate. Write a physical description, personality sketch, and personal history.	When were you wrong about something? What was it?	If I had a lot of money, I'd…	I have many things to do. I…	What are your family's holiday traditions?
What do you make or cook at home? Describe how you make it.	What do you remember about last winter vacation?	Write some new polite ways to answer your phone at home.	Tell about a movie you saw and why you liked or disliked it.	What do you hope to do in the new year?

Name _____   Skill: Writing from experience

December Delights

❄ Some of the things I love about December are:

D _____
E _____
C _____
E _____
M _____
B _____
E _____
R _____

❄ Other things I love about December are:

_____
_____
_____
_____

❄ My favorite thing about December is
_____

because _____
_____
_____
_____

Brainwork! Make a holiday card for a friend.

JANUARY

Monday	Tuesday	Wednesday	Thursday	Friday
The best part of winter vacation was...	This year I am looking forward to...	Describe a special present you received.	Write a grammar poem using: One noun _____ Two adjectives _____ Three verbs _____ One phrase _____ Write three more.	I had an argument with someone. Explain.
What do you like to do with your family?	Relate a conversation you took part in.	I am proud of something I did for someone else. I...	Write a letter to your parents telling them what you've learned recently in social studies.	If you could change something about your school, what would it be?
What routine do you follow when getting up in the morning and getting ready for school?	How do you spend your time after school?	What qualities do you have that make you a good friend?	Write ten things you'd like to do when you are an adult.	How do you know when something is right or wrong?
How did you learn to ride a bicycle? Who helped you learn?	What one thing would you change about yourself if you could? Why?	Write about a time when you felt you were left out of a group.	Describe your favorite winter activity.	Write as many funny ways as you can for using a wastepaper basket.

© Frank Schaffer Publications, Inc.

FS-32012 Writing

FEBRUARY

Monday	Tuesday	Wednesday	Thursday	Friday
What book character would you most like to be? Explain your choice.	Describe some creative, fun ways to celebrate winter.	What is your homework routine?	Describe from memory the front door of your house.	In school I do best when...
How was your weekend? Write about it in detail.	Cold weather can be unpleasant when...	What do you consider the most important quality in a friend? Give examples.	Write a friend's name. Use each letter as the first letter of a line of a poem describing your friend.	What makes your best friend *your* best friend? Describe some fun times you've had together.
What three things do you own that you treasure most? Why?	Describe the last few times you laughed.	Change the ending of a story you have read.	What is one thing you want to learn how to do better? Why?	If I become a parent, I would like to...
The kind of teacher I like best is one who...	Write a compliment you have given or received. Write three compliments you'd like to give.	Name a person you are glad to know. Give reasons for your answer.	How many ways can you think of to make this class a happier, more enjoyable place?	How did you first learn to jump rope or roller skate? How would you help someone else?

Name _____   Skill: Writing about values

Valentine Values

In each section write about something or someone you value.

Brainwork! Choose one section and write more about it.

© Frank Schaffer Publications, Inc.   FS-32012 Writing

MARCH

Monday	Tuesday	Wednesday	Thursday	Friday
A boy my age ran up to me and asked for help. He said he couldn't remember who he was or where he lived. Complete the story.	Think of an author you would like to interview. List three questions you would ask him or her.	Adjectives / Nouns Muddy / footprint A R C H Use in a story.	The Clock That Ran Backwards	Write about the marvelous things your hands help you do.
Think of a situation in which a kite could cause trouble. Write a story about it.	It is boring to…because…	Spring to me means kites…	Replace words in book and movie titles with synonyms. "Star Wars" "Planet Battles"	How to Give a Great Party
St. Patrick's Day is March 17—a day to wear green. Write a list of things that are green.	If you could solve any problem, what would it be? How would you solve it? Why do you need to solve it?	Select one word that friends would use to describe you. Explain.	Let's celebrate spring by…	What would you do if the electricity went out one night when you were home alone?
My home is…	Write and answer questions about a subject you're studying. Begin with the words *who, what, when, where* and *how*.	Invent a contest. Describe the rules and give examples.	Write different ways to move, such as *march* and *run*. Use each in a sentence.	Invent something. What would it do?

© Frank Schaffer Publications, Inc.

FS-32012 Writing

Name _____ Skill: Writing a story

A Prickly Worm

Combine an adjective and a noun in an unusual way to create new creatures or objects. Use your new creatures, including "a prickly worm," and objects in a story.

Adjectives	Nouns
prickly	worm

Brainwork! Illustrate your story.

APRIL

Monday	Tuesday	Wednesday	Thursday	Friday
Write fun, harmless ways to trick someone on April Fool's Day.	In your own words, rewrite a paragraph from a book.	Write an April poem. A time for showers A P R I L	If you could be any age, how old would you be and why?	___ is the best day of the week because...
An antonym is a word meaning the opposite of another. Use five pairs of antonyms in a story.	Dear Abby, I have a problem (real or imaginary)...	Tell about something beautiful to you.	The whole horizon was covered by a dark cloud...	Yesterday...
Write a story using direct quotes. Instead of *said*, use words such as *gasped* or *blurted*.	What can teachers do to make learning more fun?	Suddenly the flashlight went out...	Describe a member of your family.	"My Pet" or "The Pet I Wish I Had"
Describe a time you felt proud of yourself.	I like to go...	If you could meet any person in the world, whom would you want to meet and why?	Daydreams	The most trouble I ever got into was...

Name _____   Skill: **Writing from experience**

What is your favorite sport or game?

How did you learn to play it?

PLAY BALL!

What are the rules?

Why do you like it?

My Favorite Sport or Game

_____
_____
_____
_____
_____
_____
_____
_____
_____
_____
_____

Brainwork! Continue your essay on the back of this paper.

MAY

Monday	Tuesday	Wednesday	Thursday	Friday
May Day is a celebration of spring. Describe how your class might celebrate it.	Why is it important to you to get good grades?	What is something you can do quite well? Explain.	What present would you give your mother? Why would she like it?	Describe different ways you would try to communicate in a foreign country.
May I...? Write **ten** questions starting with *May you* you could ask a friend, parent, or teacher.	What makes you smile?	My favorite thing about my mother is...	My favorite experiences with mom...	Think of a story character you would like for a friend. Give reasons for your choice.
If you had two hours to spend with a friend, what would you do?	Write about a time when you got lost or when you lost something.	Write a paragraph that explains how to peel an orange.	Write friendly welcome-home notes to your mom, dad, or others in your family.	My worst day....
May—Yam Write a word that spells something forward and backward. Use it in a story.	You are walking along the beach and see a bottle floating in the water. If it contains a message that says...	My Thoughts About Horses	If you wrote a book today, what would be the title? What would it be about?	What TV show might be fun for a family to watch together? Why?

JUNE

Monday	Tuesday	Wednesday	Thursday	Friday
Describe what you'd think and do if you were alone on a deserted island for one week.	Write a thank-you note to your teacher. Tell him or her the things you like about the class.	Look at the world around you. What is something you wonder about?	Describe a perfect secret hideaway. Where would it be? What would be inside?	Summer vacation will be here soon! Plan an imaginary trip you'd like to take.
How do you pass the time on long car trips?	If you could learn a new skill, what would it be? Why would you like to learn it?	Four People on a Raft	Under his pillow, Howie found a note saying...	Father's Day is coming soon. Write your dad a letter recalling some happy times together.
This summer...	What are some fun things to do without spending a cent?	Write about one thing you learned in school this month.	Write a letter to the person who will be sitting at your desk in September. Tell that person about your class.	How do you think you learn best?
What things in nature do you love the most?	Your sailboat is caught in a storm in the middle of a lake.	What were the highlights and low points of the past school year?	Which subject did you like most this year? Why?	Some new things I might try this summer are...

Name _____   Skill: Recalling and describing the past

Reflections on Fourth Grade

Name _____   Skill: Evaluating

 # Weekly Review

1. What topic did you especially enjoy writing about this week? _____
   _____

   Why? _____
   _____

2. What creative writing assignment do you feel was your best?
   _____

3. Why do you think it's your best work?
   _____
   _____

4. Write one of your favorite sentences from that assignment.
   _____
   _____

5. How could you have made it even better?
   _____
   _____
   _____

6. What is the most important thing you were trying to say to the reader? _____
   _____
   _____

7. What has happened this past week that you would like to write about? Write it on the back of this paper.

© Frank Schaffer Publications, Inc.   FS-32012 Writing

Name _____ Skill: Sequencing directions

What Did You Say to Do First?

Did you ever get lost following someone's directions? If you want someone to understand your directions or instructions, write them in a step-by-step order. Words such as *first*, *next*, *then*, and *finally* help make directions easy to follow. They are called **order words**.

These steps for brushing your teeth are mixed up. Number the steps in their correct sequence. Then use order words and write the steps in paragraph form.

_____ Brush down on your top teeth and up on your bottom teeth.

_____ Put your toothpaste and toothbrush away.

_____ Get out your toothbrush and toothpaste.

_____ Rinse your mouth and toothbrush with water.

_____ Squeeze toothpaste on your toothbrush.

_____ Wet the toothpaste on your toothbrush.

_____
_____
_____
_____
_____
_____

Draw a sequence of six pictures to show the steps above.

Brainwork! Write directions for something you do the same way every day.

Name _____ Skill: Sequencing directions

Daffy Directions

Number these daffy directions in their correct order so you could follow them (if you were silly enough).

A. How to Pretend You're a Rock

_____ Second, crouch down beside the sidewalk.

_____ Tuck your head down so your face doesn't show.

_____ If they don't say hello, you've fooled them!

_____ First, go outside when it's almost dark.

_____ When you hear people walking by you, don't make a sound.

B. How to Catch a Galoop

_____ Begin by dressing in red and yellow to attract Galoops.

_____ The Galoop will be startled and jump high in the sky.

_____ Then carry your jar to a field and wait.

_____ Secondly, make sure you have a Galoop-catching jar.

_____ When he lands, snatch the Galoop in your jar.

_____ When you see a Galoop, yell, "Boo, Galoop!"

Now write six-step directions on "How to Get to My House From Mars."

_____
_____
_____
_____
_____
_____

Brainwork! Write five-step directions for something silly. Mix the order of your sentences and give them to a friend to sequence.

Name _____ Skill: Sequencing directions

Pretty As a Picture

It's hard to write directions so that anyone can draw what you have in mind. The directions below are not very clear. Try to follow them and draw each step in the box. When you are done, compare your picture with a classmate's.

Draw a V. Connect the tops of the V with a line. Start at one corner and draw half a circle. Draw another circle on top of the first one. Add dots. Then put a circle on top.

The directions were for drawing an ice cream cone with two scoops, chocolate sprinkles on the ice cream, and a cherry on the top. Write better directions for drawing this picture. Then follow your directions and draw each step in the box.

Brainwork! Write directions for drawing a circle, square, triangle, or rectangle. Have a classmate follow your directions to draw the shape.

Name _____   Skill: Sequencing directions

Mystery Drawings

In the box on the right draw a simple picture or diagram.

.... fold line ....

Write simple, step-by-step directions explaining exactly how to draw your picture.

_____
_____
_____
_____
_____
_____
_____
_____

Now fold your picture back on the fold line so your drawing is hidden. Exchange papers with a classmate. Drawing in the box, follow each other's directions. Have your classmate sign his or her name.

_____
Classmate's signature

Brainwork! Compare your classmate's picture with your original drawing. Circle in blue any differences in your classmate's picture. Rewrite the directions to better explain the circled areas.

© Frank Schaffer Publications, Inc.   FS-32012 Writing

Name _____ Skill: Creative writing, Sequencing directions

How Should I Start?

Here's a chance to write directions for making something real or imaginary. Complete each title below. Then write directions on the lines. Use the order words to start your sentences.

How to Train a _____

First, _____
_____

Then, _____
_____

Next, _____
_____

Finally, _____
_____
_____

Make Your Own _____

To begin, _____
_____
_____

After that, _____
_____
_____

Later, _____
_____

Lastly, _____
_____

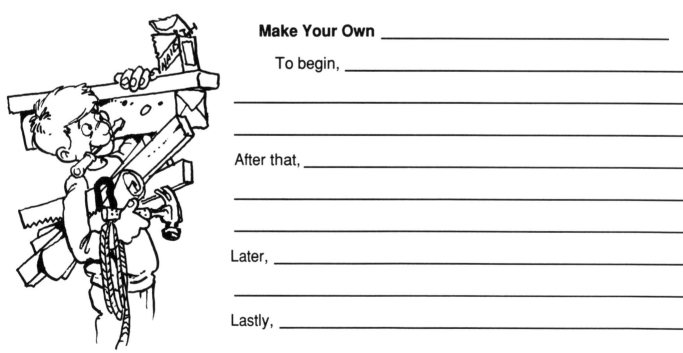

Brainwork! Write directions for playing your favorite game. Begin by listing the equipment needed.

Name _____ Skill: Creative writing, Sequencing directions

Invent a Machine

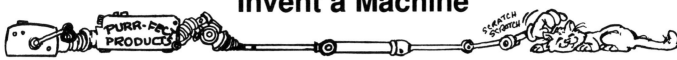

Invent a machine that will make life easier for people such as a homework machine, bread-buttering mechanism, or dog-walking device. First, draw a picture of your invention in the box. Then, write step-by-step directions explaining how to use it.

Directions

The name of my machine is _____

_____

This is how to use it. First, _____

_____
_____
_____
_____
_____
_____
_____
_____
_____
_____
_____
_____
_____
_____
_____
_____

Brainwork! Write a story about someone who used your invention. Tell how it worked. Use order words such as *first*, *next*, or *then* to help you sequence the events in your story.

Name _____   Skill: Sequencing actions

First, Second, Third...

Many things you do are done the same way every time. Do you wake up, eat breakfast, go to school, and then go home? Most students do these things in this order, although some students may say they wake up after they eat breakfast!

Decide the usual sequence for each set of actions below. Write the numbers 1 through 4 on each set of blanks to show what happens first, second, third, and fourth.

Set A
_____ Spread butter on the toast.
_____ Put the bread in the toaster.
_____ Get out a slice of bread.
_____ Eat the toast.

Set B
_____ Pick up the bat.
_____ Run to first base.
_____ Hit the ball to left field.
_____ Swing the bat.

Draw a sequence of four pictures that show how to make a peanut butter and jelly sandwich. Write a sentence under each picture to describe it.

1. _____

2. _____

3. _____

4. _____

Brainwork! Compare your sequence of pictures with a classmate's. Describe the differences.

Name _____   Skill: Sequencing actions

What Do I Do First?

Decide the usual sequence for each set of actions below. Write the numbers 1 through 4 on each set of blanks to show what happens first, second, third, and fourth.

Set A

____ Bake the cake.

____ Mix the cake batter.

____ Frost the cake.

____ Pour the batter in a pan.

Set B

____ Get into the pool.

____ Dry yourself with a towel.

____ Swim a few laps.

____ Put on your swimsuit.

Choose one of the activities above. Using a sequence of six actions, write a different way to do it.

1. _____
2. _____
3. _____
4. _____
5. _____
6. _____

Now think of something you usually do the same way every time. Write a sequence of four steps that describe your actions.

1. _____
2. _____
3. _____
4. _____

Brainwork! Draw a sequence of pictures for one of the activities above.

Name _____

Skill: Sequencing events

How Did It Happen?

Each row of pictures tells a story, but the pictures are out of order! In the boxes, number the pictures in each row in the correct sequence. Then under each picture, write a sentence describing what is happening.

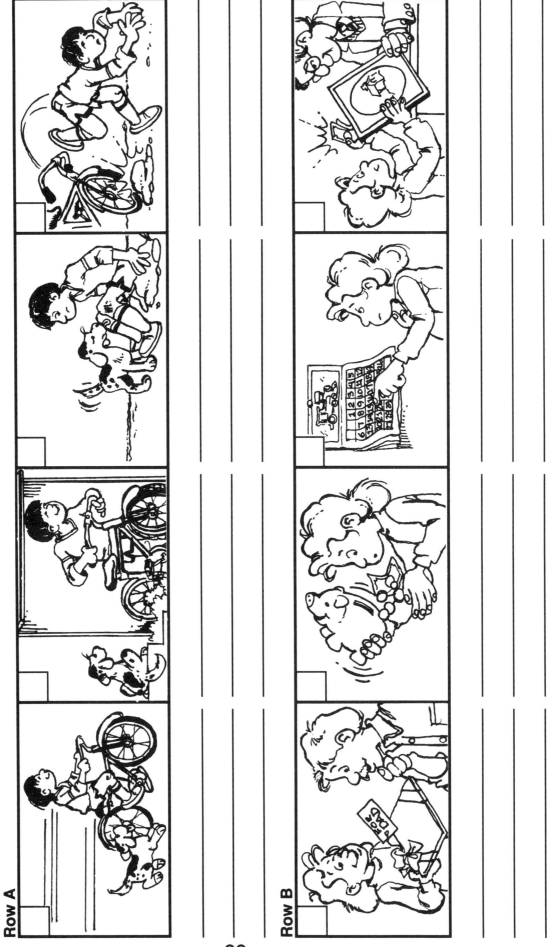

Brainwork! Tell a story by drawing four pictures in sequence. Write a sentence under each picture to describe what is happening.

Name _____   Skill: Sequencing events

The Beginning, Middle, and End

Think of an experience you have had, such as a terrific birthday party or a bicycle accident. When you tell a friend about it, you usually describe how the event began, what happened next, and how it ended. Your retelling has a beginning, a middle, and an end.

The paragraphs below describe an experience, but they are out of order. Write the paragraphs in the correct sequence.

A Different Dessert

I ordered my favorite dinner—a hot turkey sandwich, peas, and mashed potatoes. It was so delicious that when the waiter asked what I wanted for dessert, I said, "More potatoes, please."

When I was four years old, my parents said I could order dinner for myself! Since it was my first time, I was bursting with excitement.

My family giggled. I was so embarrassed that my face turned bright red. Even though my stomach wanted more, I told the waiter I had changed my mind and said, "I'm too full, thank you."

_____
_____
_____
_____
_____
_____
_____
_____
_____
_____
_____
_____

Brainwork! Write about one of your own experiences. Use three paragraphs to tell the beginning, middle, and end of the experience.

Name _____ Skill: Sequencing events

An Adventure Thriller!

Plan an adventure that has three different scenes, or places where events happen. Draw your scenes in order inside the boxes. Describe what happens in each scene in a separate paragraph.

1	2	3

_____
_____
_____
_____
_____
_____
_____
_____
_____
_____
_____
_____
_____

Brainwork! With classmates, act out each scene above for the rest of the class.

Name _____

Write about your own day or interview a friend.

A DAY IN THE LIFE OF _____

When I first get up I _____

_____
_____
_____
_____
_____
_____
_____
_____
_____
_____
_____
_____

Very interesting.

Name _____ Skill: Remembering a sequence of events

Summer Day Camp

As you read about Carlos's first day at summer day camp, try to remember what he did first, next, and so on.

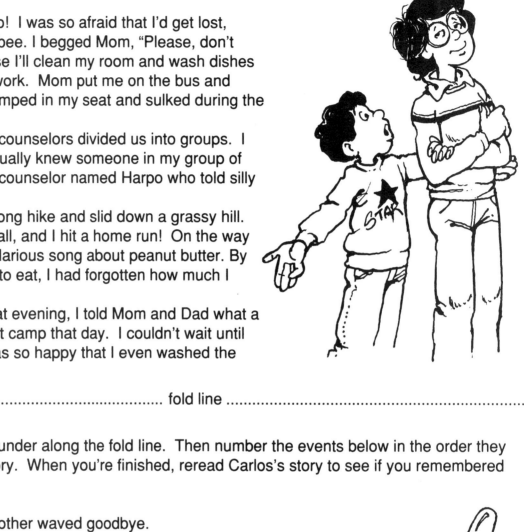

I didn't want to go! I was so afraid that I'd get lost, teased, or stung by a bee. I begged Mom, "Please, don't make me go! I promise I'll clean my room and wash dishes every night!" It didn't work. Mom put me on the bus and waved goodbye. I slumped in my seat and sulked during the ride to day camp.

After our arrival, counselors divided us into groups. I was amazed that I actually knew someone in my group of nine guys. We had a counselor named Harpo who told silly jokes.

First, we took a long hike and slid down a grassy hill. Next, we played softball, and I hit a home run! On the way to lunch, we sang a hilarious song about peanut butter. By the time we sat down to eat, I had forgotten how much I hated summer camp.

During dinner that evening, I told Mom and Dad what a great time I had had at camp that day. I couldn't wait until tomorrow. In fact I was so happy that I even washed the dishes!

.... fold line ....

Fold Carlos's story under along the fold line. Then number the events below in the order they happened in the story. When you're finished, reread Carlos's story to see if you remembered correctly.

_____ His mother waved goodbye.

_____ Carlos was so happy about camp that he did the dishes!

_____ Carlos begged his mother not to make him go to camp.

_____ Carlos was placed in a group of nine boys with a counselor named Harpo.

_____ The campers sang a silly song about peanut butter.

_____ The campers went hiking and played baseball.

_____ Carlos forgot how much he hated camp.

_____ Carlos was quiet on the ride to camp.

Brainwork! Write about a special day you remember. Arrange the events in the order they occurred.

Name _____

Skill: Sequencing events

When Did It Happen?

Each row of pictures tells a story, but the pictures are out of order! In the boxes, number the pictures in each row in the correct sequence. Then under each picture, write a sentence describing what is happening.

Row A

Row B

Brainwork! Write a story to go with one row of pictures above. Add details, dialogue, and your own ending.

Name _____ Skill: Sequence by time

Out of Order

When you write events in a story describing what happens first, next, and so on, you are ordering your sentences by **time**.

Below is a story with two events. Read the sentences in each event. Then in the boxes, number the sentences in the order they happened.

Event A

☐ I must have grown wings overnight!

☐ When I woke up today, I felt a little funny.

☐ I reached back to scratch the itch.

☐ I had an itchy feeling on my back.

☐ When I touched my back, I felt something strange.

Event B

☐ My reflection had small, white, feathery wings.

☐ I looked in the mirror to see my back.

☐ Now that I knew they worked, I longed to fly.

☐ Carefully, I wiggled my shoulders to see if my wings worked.

☐ I flapped my wings back and forth and began my first flight.

Choose one event from the story above to write in paragraph form. Write the sentences in the correct sequence.

_____
_____
_____
_____
_____
_____

Brainwork! Write a five-sentence paragraph that tells what happened next in the story above. Illustrate it.

Name _____   Skill: Sequencing sentences

Silly Sequence

The sentences in each paragraph below are out of order. Read each paragraph. In the boxes, number the sentences in the proper order. Finally, write the paragraphs so the sentences are in the correct sequence.

Paragraph A

☐ First of all, worms have a lot of protein per ounce. ☐ Secondly, worms are easy to raise. ☐ Why would you ever say, "Please pass the worms"? ☐ Therefore, many scientists see them as a very nutritious food for the future.

_____
_____
_____
_____
_____
_____

Paragraph B

☐ Do you know the song most often sung in America? ☐ The next clue is that people sing it to you on one day of the year. ☐ The first clue is that you probably sing it several times a year. ☐ If you have guessed "Happy Birthday," you are right! ☐ The third clue is that it was even sung in space by the Apollo IX astronauts.

_____
_____
_____
_____
_____
_____

Brainwork! Write a four-sentence paragraph telling why you **wouldn't** eat worms. Mix up your sentences and give them to a classmate to sequence.

Name _____ Skill: Sequencing sentences

More Silly Sequence

The sentences in the paragraphs below are out of order. Read each paragraph. In the boxes, number the sentences in the proper order. Finally, write the paragraphs so the sentences are in the correct sequence.

Paragraph A

☐ Then he reached into his hat and pulled out a scared rabbit. ☐ Morris the Magician greeted the crowd. ☐ Suddenly, the rabbit took off into the audience! ☐ First, he took off his hat and bowed deeply. ☐ Poor Morris ran after him.

_____
_____
_____
_____
_____
_____

Paragraph B

☐ For breakfast she eats only cereal. ☐ Finally, Tinker won't go to sleep until I pull her blanket over her. ☐ My cat Tinker thinks she's human! ☐ After she has eaten, someone must bring her a dab of toothpaste to lick! ☐ First, Tinker won't get up until my alarm buzzes.

_____
_____
_____
_____
_____
_____

Brainwork! Choose one story from above. Draw a picture for each sentence.

Name _____   Skill: Sequencing within paragraphs

We Need Some Order!

Sometimes a paragraph is a sequence of actions that describe an event. Each group of sentences below tells about one event, but the sentences are out of sequence. In paragraph form, write each group of sentences in the correct order.

1. While they were waiting for the bus, it began to rain.
   They wished they had brought their umbrellas.
   Sal and Mario walked to the bus stop.

   _____
   _____
   _____
   _____
   _____

2. A huge, green, scaly monster climbed in my window!
   Then, it gobbled up all my homework.
   First, it grabbed my pencil and eraser.

   _____
   _____
   _____
   _____
   _____
   _____

3. When she wakes up, she wishes the dog were real.
   Janice has had the same dream every night this week.
   It's about a furry dog that talks to her.

   _____
   _____
   _____
   _____
   _____

Brainwork! For each paragraph above, add your own ending sentence.

Name _____   Skill: Sequencing sentences for two paragraphs

The Tweedles on Conox

The sentences below form two paragraphs—three sentences describe creatures called Tweedles and three sentences describe where they live. On the first blank beside each sentence, write a **C** if it describes the creatures and an **L** if it describes where they live.

Next, reread the six sentences. Number the **C** sentences **1**, **2**, or **3** in the correct sequence. Then number the **L** sentences in the correct sequence. Write the sentences in order to form two paragraphs.

_C_ _1_   Tweedles are tiny purple creatures.

____ ____   The pull of gravity is weak on this planet.

____ ____   They have small spindly legs, webbed feet, and large round heads.

____ ____   Tweedles inhabit the green planet Conox.

____ ____   Because of this, buildings need to be tied down so they won't float away.

____ ____   Their heads are large because they have huge brains.

Brainwork! Write a third paragraph describing a school on Conox.

Name _____   Skill: Sequencing within paragraphs

Follow the Leader

If a paragraph describes an event, the first sentence usually introduces it. The sentences that follow describe only that event.

The six sentences below need to be divided into two paragraphs. Three sentences describe a downhill skier's experience. Write an **S** in the box by each sentence that describes the skier. Three sentences tell about an outerspace visitor's adventure on the earth. Write a **V** in the box by each sentence that describes the visitor.

☐ 1. Her heart pounded as she crossed the finish line.

☐ 2. She landed on the desert.

☐ 3. Walking down the steps, she prepared herself to meet humans.

☐ 4. As she raced toward her first turn, snow swirled around her.

☐ 5. At the sound of the gun, she skied down the hill.

☐ 6. After landing, she opened the door to peer outside.

The sentences that describe the event often tell what happened first, next, and so on. Reread each group of sentences above. Using paragraph form, write each group of sentences in the correct sequence. You will have two paragraphs when you're finished.

A. Downhill Skier

_____
_____
_____
_____

B. Earth Visitor

_____
_____
_____
_____

Brainwork! For one of the paragraphs above, write a second paragraph that adds another episode to the event. Illustrate your episode.

Name _____   Skill: Sequencing details

This Calls for Details

A paragraph often begins with a **topic sentence** that tells the main idea. Other sentences give supporting details that tell more about the main idea. Sometimes words like *first, second, next, also, then,* and *finally* are used to arrange the details in a certain order.

For each paragraph below, the topic sentence is given. Your challenge is to finish each paragraph by ordering and writing supporting details. Choose your details from the Supporting Details List. Mark a check in each box as you use a detail.

Supporting Details List

☐ First of all, there are no books!

☐ Second, a young duckbill drinks its mother's milk like a mammal.

☐ Scientists have filled this library with seeds from rare plants that may someday die out.

☐ And finally, it has a snout like the bill of a duck.

☐ Then if these plants do die out, scientists can grow them once again using their library of seeds.

☐ First, it lays eggs like a bird.

A.
There is a library in Mexico that's very different. _____
_____
_____
_____
_____
_____

B.
The duckbill platypus is a strange animal. _____
_____
_____
_____
_____

Brainwork! Write a paragraph about a favorite pet or animal. Start with a topic sentence. Use supporting details.

Name _____ Date _____ Topic Sentences

Terrific Topics

Every paragraph has a topic sentence. It often appears as the first sentence of a paragraph, but not always. That's up to the writer. What the topic sentence must say is what the paragraph will be about. It gives the main idea of the paragraph. Look at the paragraph below written by Jeff. The topic sentence has been underlined for you.

Unseated from a Unicycle

<u>I always wanted to learn how to ride a unicycle.</u> When my friend Jan got one for her birthday, I couldn't wait to try it! I went to Jan's house. She let me have a turn. I hopped on the unicycle and fell right off. I had thought it would be easy to ride. I fell off at least twenty times. Jan was laughing. I didn't mind because I wasn't hurt. Finally, after several hours, I mastered it. I'm going to ask Mom and Dad for one for my birthday.

Write a paragraph telling whether or not Jeff got his own unicycle, why or why not, and what happened. Underline the topic sentence.

★**Brainwork!** Would you like to have a unicycle? Why or why not?

Name _____ Date _____ Paragraph Writing: Getting Started

Perfect Paragraphs

Writing paragraphs is easy if you remember these important steps: 1. Decide what you want to write about and stick to it in that paragraph. 2. Always indent when you begin a paragraph. 3. Only use complete sentences. 4. Don't make your paragraph too long. If it is, you may really need two paragraphs. 5. Use a variety of words. 6. Don't say the same thing over and over again.

Look at the sample paragraph. Draw a line under the sentence that should begin a new paragraph. Draw two lines under the sentence that tells what the first paragraph is about.

Lost in the Library

<u>When I go to the library I never like to leave</u>. The library is one of my favorite places in the world. It has books about everything I like. I can read about animals, faraway places, and how to build things. My mother says I get lost in the library when she takes me there. <u>Once I found a book about building birdhouses</u>. I found a birdhouse that I thought the birds in my neighborhood would like. I made it all by myself from wood scraps in the garage. Birds live in it all year around, now. Mom says they fly south just to live in my birdhouse!

Write a paragraph of your own about your favorite kind of books. Don't forget the rules above!

★**Brainwork! Make a list of the five best books you've ever read.**

Name _____ Date _____ Paragraph Writing: Fiction

Just in Time

You have just brought George Washington back from the past in your time machine. George is very confused by everything he sees. Write a paragraph. Describe something that George finds strange. Explain its use and how it works, what it does, why we need it. Remember that George lived two hundred years ago. Explain each thing very carefully so he'll understand. Choose one thing from the list below.

airplane   car   hamburgers   rock music   TV   telephone   electric lights
washing machine   supermarket   pinball

George Washington, Time Traveler

★**Brainwork! Do you think George Washington would like to stay in our time? Why or why not?**

Name _____ Date _____ Paragraph Writing: Instructions

Buy a Pet Pinecone!

Lucy heard that someone made lots of money selling rocks. They were called "Pet Rocks" and were sold in a box. Lucy has decided to sell pet pinecones. Write a paragraph with directions and suggestions for people who will buy a pet pinecone. Answer these questions when you write. Do a good job and Lucy might get rich!

1. What is a Pet Pinecone?
2. What do they look like?
3. Why should people buy one?
4. How do you take care of them?
5. What's fun about them?
6. Why are they good pets?
7. Why are they better than other pets?

Pet Pinecones

_____
_____
_____
_____
_____
_____
_____
_____

★**Brainwork!** **What do you think of Lucy's idea? Would you buy a Pet Pinecone? Why or why not? How much should they cost?**

Paragraph Writing: A Speech

Vote for Me!

Annie is running for president of her class. She needs a good, convincing speech to get people to vote for her. Annie wrote notes on what she wants to say in her speech. These are her notes:

Tell my classmates:
1) Who I am
2) Why I want to be president
3) What I will do for the class
4) Why everyone should vote for me.

I should not:
1) Make promises I can't keep
2) Say mean things about my opponents
3) Use too many "I"s or "and"s when I speak

DON'T FORGET!! ➔ Speak in complete sentences, and speak correctly!

Using Annie's notes, write a speech for her in one paragraph. Do the best you can, because you really want Annie to win, don't you?

_____
_____
_____
_____
_____
_____
_____
_____
_____
_____
_____
_____

★Brainwork! Would you like to be president of your class? Why or why not?

"I'm Jason's Room."

When Jason's dad helps his son clean his room, he says to Jason, "This room is a mess, a pigpen. No, I take that back. Pigs would be ashamed to live here! Jason, if this room could talk, it would tell you how it feels about being treated this way! I bet it hates being cluttered, dusty, messy, and dirty. If only the furniture, walls, and floor could talk. I bet the closet would have a thing or two to say, too!" Jason thought about what Dad had said.

Pretend Jason's room can talk. Write this paragraph in the first person. That means that Jason's room will talk about itself and how it feels. The room will always refer to itself as "I." Read the paragraph above to remember how Jason's room looks. Think of how you would feel if you looked that way!

I'm Jason's room. My name is Robbie. I _____

_____

_____

_____

_____

_____

_____

_____

_____

★**Brainwork!** What would your room say if it could talk?

Name _____ Date _____ Paragraph Writing

We'll Be Back After This Important Message

Have you ever seen a commercial on TV and thought, "Boy, is that silly. I could write a better one than that!" Here's your chance. There's a brand new product that every boy and girl your age will love. It's called, "Instant Sundae." All you do is pour out the contents of a box into a dish. Add water and before your very eyes the mixture turns into a fudge or butterscotch sundae complete with topping, cherry, and nuts! Best of all, "Instant Sundae" is healthful and contains no chemicals or preservatives. Parents won't mind if children eat "Instant Sundae." This delicious new product is available in vanilla or chocolate flavored ice cream, with butterscotch or fudge topping. It only costs fifty-nine cents.

Using the facts above, write a TV commercial in one paragraph that will make people want to buy "Instant Sundae." Your commercial must be clear, convincing, and interesting.

It's New! Instant Sundae!

★**Brainwork! Write a commercial for a new game, toy, book, or bike. Be convincing!**

Name _____ Date _____ Paragraphs: Description

My Town

Mrs. Philpot and her class were discussing the places in which they were born. Most of the students were from the town they were in now, Blissburg. Mrs. Philpot told everyone about her hometown, Rainbow Ridge. She described it so well and so clearly that when she was done, most of the class wanted to visit or even live in Rainbow Ridge. This is what Mrs. Philpot said:

"I lived in a large white house on a tree-shaded street. After school my friends would often play at my house. My mom would have cookies and lemonade for us, or hot chocolate in the cold weather. The school was only four blocks away. A stream ran right by it. When the weather was warm, we'd take off our shoes and socks. At recess we'd wade in the stream. In winter, we could ice skate in that same stream, too. On weekends, families would go on picnics in the nearby hills. In spring those hills were covered with wildflowers. Rainbow Ridge had two movie theatres, a small department store, a grocery, and a few other stores. Everyone was proud of our little town and kept it clean and neat."

Write a description of your town or city in one paragraph. Don't forget to mention places, people, and what you do in your town for fun. You can also write about the good and bad things about your town.

My Town

_____
_____
_____
_____
_____
_____
_____
_____
_____
_____

★Brainwork! Write a paragraph about the town or neighborhood of your dreams.

Name _____ Date _____ Friendly Letter

Making Friends

A friendly letter is composed of five parts: the heading, greeting, body, closing, and signature. When you write a letter, make it lively and tell the person to whom you are writing things about yourself and what you are doing. Don't forget to ask your friend or relative questions about what he or she is doing too. That way, you'll be more likely to get a letter back! Hint: the best way to receive letters is to write them first!

Laura wrote a letter to her new pen pal in Australia. She wanted to tell her new friend about herself, her family and home. Read Laura's letter. Pretend you have a pen pal in another country. Write him or her a friendly letter using the same form that Laura used.

>235 Green Street
>North Hollywood, California 91605
>June 12, 1982

Dear Marnie,

    My name is Laura Levin. I am ten years old. I am in the fifth grade at Green Street School. I have a brother and a sister. I also have parents and a dog. I like to skateboard, roller skate and ride my bike. I love to go to the movies. My favorite foods are pizza and hot fudge sundaes.

    I don't know much about Australia. Do you have a pet kangaroo or koala bear? What do you learn in school? What grade are you in? Do you have brothers and sisters? Please write to me soon.

>Your new friend,
>Laura Levin

Now write your letter. Choose: your pen pal's country, what you want to say about yourself, and what you want to know about your new friend.

_____
_____
_____

_____

_____
_____
_____
_____
_____

_____
_____

Name _____ Date _____ Friendly Letter

Hello and Goodbye

We usually begin a friendly letter with "Dear" and end it with "Sincerely," or "Yours truly." But there are many ways to begin and end letters. If you are writing to a close friend or relative, you might want to sound a lot friendlier. Write a letter to your very best friend or to your mom or dad. First, list all the greetings that you might use, then the closings. A few are already listed to get you started. Then, write a letter on the form below.

Greetings	**Closings**
1. Dearest	1. Your loving son (or daughter)
2. Hi!	2. Your best friend
3. Hello there	3. See you
4. _____	4. _____
5. _____	5. _____
6. _____	6. _____
7. _____	7. _____
8. _____	8. _____

© Frank Schaffer Publications, Inc. FS-32012 Writing

Name _____ Date _____ Friendly Letter: Thank-you Note

Thanks a Lot!

Ruth sure had gotten lots of birthday presents! The day after her party, she was putting all her new things in her room. Dad came in. He said, "You're going to have to write thank you notes to each person who sent you a gift." Ruth groaned. Then she smiled. "That's easy," she said. "I'll just write the same note to everyone and say, "Thanks for the gift. It is very nice. Love, Ruth." But Dad said that each person had to be thanked separately and each gift mentioned. Write two thank you notes for Ruth. One should be for the dollhouse that her grandmother sent her. The other is for the toy typewriter that her friend Billy gave her. She should tell both people how she feels about their gifts, what she is going to do with them, and how much she appreciates their thoughtfulness.

Dear Grandma,

_____

_____

_____

_____

                                                                                     Love,
                                                                                    Ruth

Dear Billy,

_____

_____

_____

_____

                                                                          Your friend,
                                                                         Ruth

★**Brainwork! Write a letter to your parents or a friend, thanking them for a birthday gift.**

Name _____ Date _____ Friendly Letter Invitation

The Party

Bertha is having a birthday party. She wants to send special invitations to her friends. Below are the facts you need. Write the invitation for Bertha, using these facts. Make it interesting so everyone will want to come!

| clown | presents | ice cream | games | two o'clock | Kiddyland |
| fun | nine years old | seven-layer cake | jeans and tennis shoes |

Come For Birthday Fun!

_____
_____
_____
_____
_____
_____

David can't come to Bertha's party. He wrote a note to explain. Using the words in the word box, write David's note to Bertha.

| measles | Cousin Dwayne | present | cake | big red spots |
| happy birthday | fever | next week | fun | party hats |

_____
_____
_____
_____
_____
_____

★**Brainwork!** Write a birthday or other party invitation to your friends!

Name _____ Date _____ Addressing An Envelope

Many letters are never delivered because the envelopes are addressed incorrectly. Look at the sample envelope. What makes it correct? 1. The handwriting is clear. 2. The return address appears at the top left corner of the envelope. 3. The address of the person to whom the letter was written is written large and clear. 4. The ZIP code is included. 5. Correct postage is glued to the envelope.

Using the two envelopes below, address one to a good friend and one to a favorite relative. Make sure you've remembered all the rules above.

```
Elizabeth Swann
6280 Forrest Drive
Secaucus, New Jersey    01230


              Mr. Jeffrey Powell
              943 East Washington Street
              Los Angeles, California 90068
```

© Frank Schaffer Publications, Inc. FS-32012 Writing

Name _____ Date _____ Business Letters

The Big Contest

Wow! McFeeny's Mile-High Burgers is having a big contest. The prize is a trip to the Grand Canyon or a year's supply of burgers, whichever you prefer. All you have to do is first write a new jingle for McFeeny's Burgers. It must be a short, rhyming poem of not more than four lines. Then you must color the pictures of Minton McFeeny and his burger.

Look at the old jingle. Write a business letter to McFeeny's. 1. Tell them you're submitting your entry and why you think it should win. 2. Write the jingle. 3. Color the picture. Good luck!

McFeeny's Mile-High can't be beat,
We all know they're great to eat,
Every day I want some more,
Lead me to McFeeny's door!

Name _____ Date _____ Business Letters

A Business Letter

Why write a business letter? Perhaps you are sending away for something. Maybe, as in the letter below, you have a complaint about a product. Read the letter. It includes a heading (your address), an inside address (the name and address of the person to whom you're writing), a greeting, body, closing, signature. The greeting may begin with <u>Dear, Gentlemen, Ladies and Gentlemen, Sir</u> or <u>Madam, or Sirs</u>. The closing used is usually <u>Sincerely or Yours truly.</u>

3944 Blue Sky Lane
Missoula, Montana
August 7, 1982

President
Toby Toys
81 Meadow Park
Industry, California

Dear Madam,

  Last week I bought a Space Voyage set. I am very disappointed in it. On TV you show it in action with great space noises. It really makes no noise. I have to move everything around by myself, too. I think you are fooling people. Please send my twenty-five dollars back. I have enclosed a copy of my sales slip.

Sincerely,
James Kirk
James Kirk

Write a business letter about: 1. a complaint 2. praise for a product you like 3. something you ordered that you never received.

Name _____ Date _____ Business Letter

A New Flavor

Write a business letter to Basket-Dobbins Ice Cream Company. Tell them how you feel about their bubble gum flavor. You think food flavors are a great idea for a whole line of ice creams. You want to sell them your ideas for these new taste treats. Choose one of these flavors and try to sell it to them in your business letter.
1. pepperoni pizza 2. hot dog-mustard chip 3. burger bit 4. tuna tidbit 5. candy corn. 6. chopped Milky Way.

★**Brainwork!** What is your favorite ice cream flavor? Why is it your favorite?

Name _____

Skill: Prewriting, Organizing ideas

Ideas Take Flight

Main Topic

© Frank Schaffer Publications, Inc.   57   FS-32012 Writing

Name _____   "Photo Album" Page

THREE OF MY FRIENDS

This is _____

This is _____

This is _____

Name _____

DRAW A COLOR SELF-PORTRAIT

You may need a mirror.

1. Think about your hair. Is it straight or curly? _____ dark or light? _____ long or short? _____ Does it cover your ears? _____

2. What color are your eyes? _____

3. Do you have freckles? _____

4. Think about the real you before you make the look on your face. Are you shy, funny, scared, brave or happy? Do you smile a lot? Are you often mad?

Name _____

MY NEIGHBORHOOD

Pretend you have a camera. Look around your neighborhood. Draw some pictures of interesting things you see. Look for people, pets, plants, shops, houses, signs, bugs, you-name-it! Don't forget to label the pictures!

© Frank Schaffer Publications, Inc.

FS-32012 Writing

Name _____

INTERVIEW

1. My favorite school subjects are: _____
   _____

2. A book I enjoyed is: _____

3. One hard word I can spell is: _____

4. Here is a hard math problem I can do:

5. One song I know by heart is: _____

6. Here is my best writing.

Copy this. ➡ The quick brown fox jumped over the lazy dogs.

"One more for the folks at home in TV land."

_____
_____
_____
_____

© Frank Schaffer Publications, Inc.   FS-32012 Writing

Name _____

FOODS

My favorite breakfast menu:
_____
_____
_____

My favorite lunch menu:
_____
_____
_____

My favorite dinner menu:
_____
_____
_____

Some snacks I like:
_____
_____

Name _____

THE OTHER ME

Your teacher may be curious about you. What do you do when you're not in school?

_____
_____
_____
_____
_____
_____
_____
_____
_____
_____
_____
_____

HOW DID YOU FEEL?

Once I got **mad** when _____

_____

_____

_____

Once I felt really **sad** when _____

_____

_____

_____

I was **surprised** when _____

_____

_____

_____

I was so **scared** when _____

_____

_____

_____

Name _____

WHAT'S BUGGING YOU...

1. at school? _____
   _____
   _____
   _____

2. at home? _____
   _____
   _____
   _____

3. in the world? _____
   _____
   _____
   _____

4. about yourself? _____

   _____
   _____
   _____

Name _____

MY FAVORITE TV SHOW

Draw your favorite show on the TV.

1. What is the name of the show? _____

2. When is it on? _____

3. Why do you like that show? _____
   _____

4. Is there something you do not like about TV? What is it?
   _____

5. Do you ever buy the things you see on TV commercials?
   _____

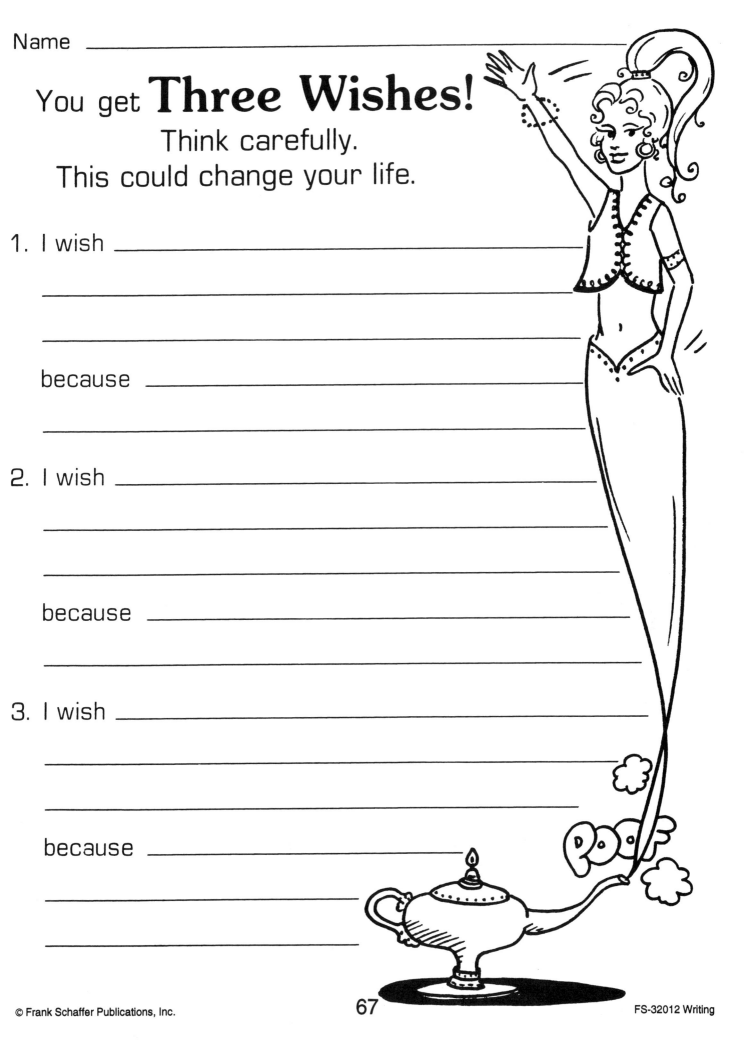

Name _____

Teachers try hard to make school interesting. They could use some help. Write down how you would change school if you were the teacher.

1. _____
_____
2. _____
_____
3. _____
_____

4. _____
_____
5. _____
_____
6. _____
_____

Name _____

You have the power to change the world! Tell five changes you'd make, and why they're important.

abra ca dabra

1. _____

   because _____

   _____

2. _____

   because _____

   _____

3. _____

   because _____

   _____

4. _____

   because _____

   _____

5. _____

   because _____

   _____

Name _____

WHEN I'M GROWN-UP

I will be honest.

Do grown-ups drive you crazy?
Well, you will be one yourself soon.
What will you be like then?

I hope I **will** be:

1. _____
2. _____
3. _____
4. _____
5. _____
6. _____
7. _____

I hope I will **not** be:

1. _____
2. _____
3. _____
4. _____
5. _____
6. _____
7. _____

© Frank Schaffer Publications, Inc.

FS-32012 Writing

Name _____

THINKING AHEAD

What will I be when I'm 23?

_____
_____
_____

What will I see when I'm 43?

_____
_____
_____

What will I do when I'm 62?

_____
_____
_____
_____

If I'm alive at 95 . . .

_____
_____
_____

Name _____

WHAT KIND OF JOB FOR ME?

I like the outdoors.

I like machines.

Fill out the checklist to help you decide.

- ☐ I want to work with people.
- ☐ I want to work with words.
- ☐ I want to work with animals.
- ☐ I want to work with children.
- ☐ I want to work with ideas.
- ☐ I want to work with machines.
- ☐ I want to work with art.
- ☐ I want to work with plants.
- ☐ I want to work with clothes.
- ☐ I want to work with books.
- ☐ I want to work with tools.
- ☐ I want to work with colors.
- ☐ I want to work with foods.
- ☐ I want to work outdoors.
- ☐ I want to work indoors.
- ☐ I like noise.
- ☐ I like quiet.
- ☐ I like excitement.
- ☐ I like calm.
- ☐ I like to talk.
- ☐ I'm shy.
- ☐ I want lots of money.

- ☐ I like to make things.
- ☐ I like to travel.
- ☐ I enjoy schoolwork.
- ☐ I don't enjoy a lot of schoolwork.
- ☐ I like to get dirty.
- ☐ I like to stay clean.
- ☐ I like danger.
- ☐ I want to be safe.
- ☐ I'm big and strong.
- ☐ I like to dress up.
- ☐ I want to live in the city.
- ☐ I'm good-looking.
- ☐ I want to live in the country.
- ☐ I want to be my own boss.
- ☐ I like music.
- ☐ I like science.
- ☐ I like math.
- ☐ I like art.
- ☐ I like to write.
- ☐ I like to read.
- ☐ I like to sell things.
- ☐ I like different things.

- ☐ I'd like to sit at a desk.
- ☐ I want to move around.
- ☐ I like to drive.
- ☐ I can take orders.
- ☐ I'm friendly.
- ☐ I'm crabby.
- ☐ I'm brave.
- ☐ I'm funny.
- ☐ I like to use my muscles.
- ☐ I like to use my mind.
- ☐ I don't need much money.
- ☐ I want to be famous.
- ☐ I want to help people.
- ☐ I like to clean.
- ☐ I like to fix things.
- ☐ I love sports.
- ☐ I get up early.
- ☐ I'm a night person.
- ☐ I like to be on my feet.
- ☐ I like to sit.
- ☐ I'm tough.
- ☐ I want lots of free time.

Circle the answers that are most important to you.

I think I'd like to be _____

Name _____

OOOOOPS!

Did you ever get in trouble? Write a little story about it. If you are perfect, you can make up a story.

_____
_____
_____
_____
_____
_____
_____
_____
_____

☐ I made this up.   ☐ This is the truth.

Name _____

Pretend you just became
A PARENT

What are your hopes and dreams for your child? Think about the parents you know . . . your own, your friends', the parents on TV. How will you be the same? How will you be different?

_____
_____
_____
_____
_____
_____
_____
_____
_____
_____
_____

Name _____

If you could drive a car, where would you go?

What would you do there?

_____
_____
_____
_____
_____
_____
_____
_____
_____
_____
_____
_____

Watch the speed limit!

Name _____

You caught a snowflake on your tongue. Describe what it tastes like and how it feels.

_____
_____
_____
_____
_____
_____
_____
_____
_____
_____
_____
_____
_____
_____

How many calories in a snowflake?

Name _____

A giant. WOW!

Write a story about your adventures as a giant.

_____
_____
_____
_____
_____
_____
_____
_____
_____
_____
_____
_____
_____
_____
_____

And my friends thought I had long legs!

Name _____

On your way home from school you find a stray hippopotamus. Try to convince your mother to let you keep him. Where will you put him? What will he eat?

_____
_____
_____
_____
_____
_____
_____
_____
_____
_____
_____
_____
_____

I'll bet your mother would like a dog better!

Name _____

You are SUPERHUMAN! Tell about your special powers and how you would use them.

I wish you could make me smell nice.

Name _____

You are at the beach playing in the sand. You dig a hole to a strange new land. Jump in and tell what you would do next.

Bye!

Now you know why an ostrich sticks his head in the sand!

Name _____

If you could visit the bottom of the ocean, what would you do down there? Write a story.

He should be in "school" today!

Name _____

Pretend that you are invisible for a day.

Write a story about what you would do.

"That's so silly!"

Name _____

...and go inside. Write about this adventure!

You climb up...

On the way home from your friend's house you find a tree house...

_____
_____
_____
_____
_____
_____
_____
_____
_____
_____
_____
_____

"No one could make me go up there!"

Name _____

Tonight you get to cook dinner. Explain exactly what you will do.

"Don't look at me. I can't cook!"

Name _____

Imagine that you have a bottle hidden in your bedroom closet. Inside the bottle live several tiny people. Write about your adventures with the little people.

_____
_____
_____
_____
_____
_____
_____
_____
_____
_____
_____
_____
_____
_____
_____
_____

How did they get in that bottle?

Name _____

Oh! There is a *lump on your blanket.*

Something is in your bed with you. Write about what it might be.

"It's not a rhino. It's probably a monster."

_____
_____
_____
_____
_____
_____
_____
_____
_____
_____
_____

Name _____

This Saturday you can go anywhere and do anything you choose. Write about some of your plans.

"Make sure you do your homework first!"

Name _____

You have been chosen to go live on the moon. What will you take with you in your suitcase?

_____
_____
_____
_____
_____
_____
_____
_____
_____
_____
_____
_____
_____
_____
_____

Hey, wait for me!

Name _____

Inside your pocket is a big secret. What is it? Where did you get it? Why is it a secret?

It's not nice to keep secrets!

Name _____

Half of an animal!??

Finish the animal and write a story about where it is going.

_____
_____
_____
_____
_____
_____
_____
_____
_____
_____
_____
_____
_____

I can tell by the ears it's not a pig.

Name _____

You won first place in a great contest! Why did you win first place? Write your story.

_____
_____
_____
_____
_____
_____
_____
_____
_____
_____
_____
_____
_____
_____

I won first place for being the most beautiful pig.

Name _____

Pretend you have eyes in the bottom of your feet. Tell about all the different things your feet would see as they walk around.

_____
_____
_____
_____
_____
_____
_____
_____
_____
_____
_____
_____
_____
_____

I don't like big feet; they step on me!

Name _____ Date _____

Directions: Think of a story to fit the pictures below. Decide what the characters should say and fill in the balloons. Then write a title for your cartoon.

Title: _____

Name _____ Date _____

Directions: Think of a story to fit the pictures below. Decide what the characters should say and fill in the balloons. Then write a title for your cartoon.

Title:

Name _____ Date _____

Directions: Think of a story to fit the pictures below. Decide what the characters should say and fill in the balloons. Then write a title for your cartoon.

Title:

Name _____ Date _____

Directions: Think of a story to fit the pictures below. Decide what the characters should say and fill in the balloons. Then write a title for your cartoon.

Title:

Name _____ Date _____

Directions: Think of a story to fit the pictures below. Decide what the characters should say and fill in the balloons. Then write a title for your cartoon.

Title:

Name _____ Date _____

Directions: Think of a story to fit the pictures below. Decide what the characters should say and fill in the balloons. Then write a title for your cartoon.

Title:

Name _____ Date _____

Directions: Think of a story to fit the pictures below. Decide what the characters should say and fill in the balloons. Then write a title for your cartoon.

Title:

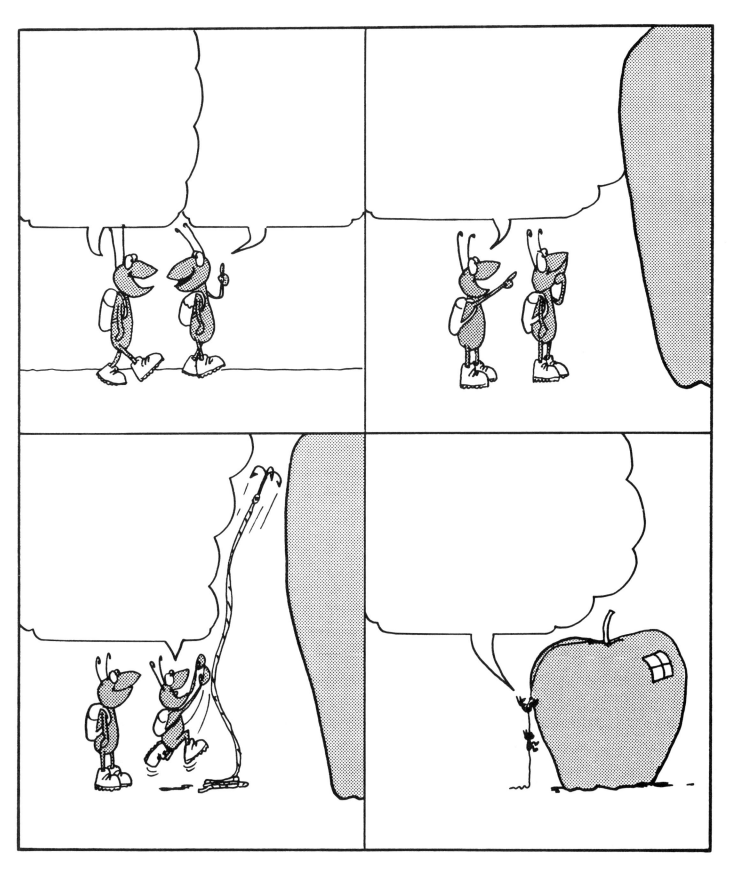

Name _____ Date _____

Directions: Think of a story to fit the pictures below. Decide what the characters should say and fill in the balloons. Then write a title for your cartoon.

Title:

© Frank Schaffer Publications, Inc.   FS-32012 Writing

Name _____ Date _____

Directions: Think of a story to fit the pictures below. Decide what the characters should say and fill in the balloons. Then write a title for your cartoon.

Title:

Name _____ Date _____

Directions: Think of a story to fit the pictures below. Decide what the characters should say and fill in the balloons. Then write a title for your cartoon.

Title:

Name _____ Date _____

Directions: Think of a story to fit the pictures below. Decide what the characters should say and fill in the balloons. Then write a title for your cartoon.

Title:

Name _____ Date _____

Directions: Think of a story to fit the pictures below. Decide what the characters should say and fill in the balloons. Then write a title for your cartoon.

Title:

Name _____ Date _____
Directions: Think of a story to fit the pictures below. Decide what the characters should say and fill in the balloons. Then write a title for your cartoon.

Title:

Name _____ Date _____

Directions: Think of a story to fit the pictures below. Decide what the characters should say and fill in the balloons. Then write a title for your cartoon.

Title:

Name _____ Date _____

Directions: Think of a story to fit the pictures below. Decide what the characters should say and fill in the balloons. Then write a title for your cartoon.

Title:

Name _____ Date _____

Directions: Think of a story to fit the pictures below. Decide what the characters should say and fill in the balloons. Then write a title for your cartoon.

Title:

Name _____ Date _____

Directions: Think of a story to fit the pictures below. Decide what the characters should say and fill in the balloons. Then write a title for your cartoon.

Title:

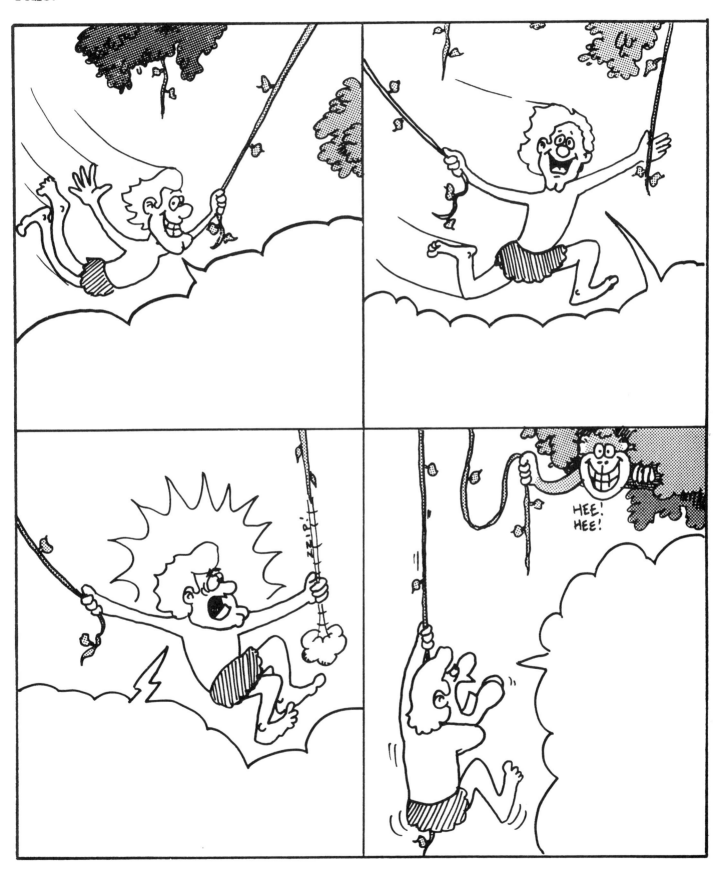

Name _____ Date _____

Directions: Think of a story to fit the pictures below. Decide what the characters should say and fill in the balloons. Then write a title for your cartoon.

Title:

Name _____ Date _____

Directions: Think of a story to fit the pictures below. Decide what the characters should say and fill in the balloons. Then write a title for your cartoon.

Title:

Name _____ **Date** _____

Directions: Think of a story to fit the pictures below. Decide what the characters should say and fill in the balloons. Then write a title for your cartoon.

Title:

Name _____ Date _____

Directions: Think of a story to fit the pictures below. Decide what the characters should say and fill in the balloons. Then write a title for your cartoon.

Title: _____

Name _____ Date _____

Directions: Think of a story to fit the pictures below. Decide what the characters should say and fill in the balloons. Then write a title for your cartoon.

Title:

Name _____ Date _____

Directions: Think of a story to fit the pictures below. Decide what the characters should say and fill in the balloons. Then write a title for your cartoon.

Title:

Name _____ Date _____

Directions: Think of a story to fit the pictures below. Decide what the characters should say and fill in the balloons. Then write a title for your cartoon.

Title:

Name _____ Date _____

Directions: Think of a story to fit the pictures below. Decide what the characters should say and fill in the balloons. Then write a title for your cartoon.

Title:

Name _____ Date _____

Directions: Think of a story to fit the pictures below. Decide what the characters should say and fill in the balloons. Then write a title for your cartoon.

Title:

Name _____ Date _____

Directions: Think of a story to fit the pictures below. Decide what the characters should say and fill in the balloons. Then write a title for your cartoon.

Title:

Name _____ Date _____

Directions: Think of a story to fit the pictures below. Decide what the characters should say and fill in the balloons. Then write a title for your cartoon.

Title:

Name _____ Date _____

Directions: Think of a story to fit the pictures below. Decide what the characters should say and fill in the balloons. Then write a title for your cartoon.

Title:

Name _____ Date _____

Directions: Think of a story to fit the pictures below. Decide what the characters should say and fill in the balloons. Then write a title for your cartoon.

Title:

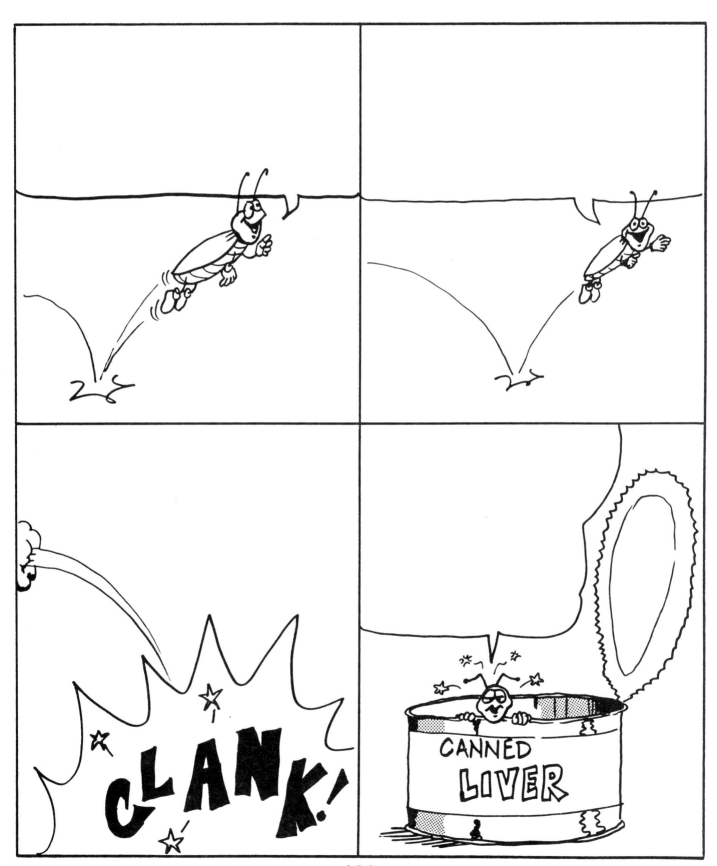

Name _____ Date _____

Directions: Think of a story to fit the pictures below. Decide what the characters should say and fill in the balloons. Then write a title for your cartoon.

Title:

Name _____ Date _____

Directions: Think of a story to fit the pictures below. Decide what the characters should say and fill in the balloons. Then write a title for your cartoon.

Title:

Name _____ Date _____ Outlines

All About Outlines

Outlines help organize your thoughts before you write a story or report. Here's how to write an outline: 1. Number the main thoughts in your report. 2. Under each main thought, write other facts about the subject.

Look at the facts below. Then look at the way they have been outlined.

The King of Beasts

The lion is commonly called the King of Beasts. One thinks of this animal as a fierce protector of his family, the killer who hunts and brings home the bacon (or the zebra) for his mate and cubs. Actually, the lioness is the member of the family who does the hunting. King Leo is usually too busy sleeping or swatting flies to pay attention to getting groceries. But when he's hungry, Mrs. Lion had better have dinner ready. A nice fat zebra, Thompson's gazelle, or giraffe is preferred. The King of Beasts eats first, then Mrs. Lion, and finally the cubs, who wrestle and fight for the choicest leftovers.

I. About the King of Beasts
   a. Lions as protectors
   b. Lions as hunters
II. The Lion Family
   a. What the lioness does
   b. What the lion does
   c. What lions eat
   d. What the cubs do

Read these facts about zebras. Organize the facts into a simple outline.

Zebras

The zebra is related to the horse, as you might suspect. It is found wild in Africa. It stands four to five feet high. It is different from other members of the horse family because of its coloring. Zebras have black or dark-brown stripes on a white background. The stripes run all over its body, even on the ears. The zebra's chief enemy is the lion. The zebra is a fierce fighter when attacked. They are sometimes tamed in South Africa, although this is hard to do.

_____
_____
_____
_____
_____
_____
_____

Name _____ Date _____ Book Reports

Rules for Reports

You can write good book reports if you are organized and follow these rules: 1. Read the whole book. 2. Tell the story of the book as briefly as possible. This can be done in one or two paragraphs. 3. Write about the most exciting or interesting part of the book. 4. Write what you thought about the book.

Read the short story below. Write a report about it using the rules above. If you run out of room, finish on the back of this paper.

The Merry Mixup

Willie quickly packed his lunch, homework, and schoolbooks. He ran for the schoolbus. Jennie was coming the other way. Crash! They bumped into each other. Lunches, books, and papers went flying in all directions. "Sorry!" said Willie. "Me, too," smiled Jennie. They hurriedly picked up all their things and got on the bus.

Later that day, Jennie took out her math homework. "Oh, no!" she gasped. "I got Willie's spelling homework by mistake!" At lunch, Jennie opened her brown lunch bag. "Not again!" she shouted. "Ick! A peanut butter sandwich!" Just then Willie came by. "I'd like my spelling and my sandwich, please. By the way, anyone who eats tomatoes and jelly is weird!" Jennie started to laugh. Willie said, "We'd both better get to the schoolbus earlier from now on!"

★Brainwork! Write a report about a book you're reading now.

Name _____ Date _____ Proofreading Symbols

Goof-Proof Writing

Understanding and correcting writing errors is easy. All you have to do is recognize and use proofreading symbols. Look at the proofreading symbols below. Read the paragraph. Notice the errors and how they're marked. Write the paragraph over correctly. Use the back of this paper for more room.

Symbol	Meaning
1. sp	Spelling is incorrect.
2. ro	run on sentence
3. ns	not a sentence
4. ¶	Start a new paragraph.
5. I	indent
6. p	incorrect punctuation
7. cap	capitalize
8. lc	should be lower case
9. ww	wrong word
10. t	wrong tense

New Shoes

I was so tired. Dad and I. we had bin in the shoe store for hours and I think I tried on every pair of shoes in there and I didn't even want shoes anymore. "I give up?" I told Dad. He sighed. Sudden, I spy the perfect pair of shoes in the corner of the Store. I jumped up grabbed them and put them on my feet. They fit! "I want these, Dad!" I yelled. Dad stood in front of me and threw his hands up in the air. "these are the shoes you came in with Danny," he said.

★**Brainwork!** Ask a friend to write a paragraph. Proofread it for him or her.

Name _____ Date _____ Proofreading

Errors Everywhere!

Was Willie embarrassed during English today! He wrote a story called "What I Want to be When I Grow Up." Willie said he wanted to be a writer. When he got his paper back, it was full of proofreading marks. That meant that Willie had made a lot of mistakes. Mrs. Fitch, his teacher, had written in the margin, "Writers check their work carefully for mistakes, Willie." Look at Willie's story. Proofread it for mistakes and insert the correct proofreading symbols. Then write the paragraph over correctly. Hint: There are fourteen errors.

Willie the Writer

Many of my friends want to be doctors, lawyers, or engineers. Some want to be teachers and police officers. But I want to be a writer. why you might ask. i no that writing is very exiting. expecially the kind I want to do. I will write for a Newspaper. I will cover fires bank robberies and dog shows. I will travel to faraway places and meet strange people I'll write strange stories and have fun. I will be the best report there is.

_____
_____
_____
_____
_____
_____
_____

★**Brainwork! Write a paragraph about your future career.**